THAT'S NOT A MOO-COW

BY JOE PATRINA AND JESSICA NOLAN

ISBN: 979-8988909415 (hc)

LittleHouse
WELCOME TO THE BARN

A CHILDREN'S LEARNING BOOK

Joe and Jess are musical partners for the country-rock band LittleHouse. Always on the lookout for fresh inspiration, Jess takes two-year-old Luke to his first country fair.

Jess calls a donkey a moo-cow, and Luke defiantly stands his ground shaking his head "no." Together they find out what animals Luke knows, and it is just a handful. So we write the book.

That's Not a Moo-Cow is designed for children age 2 to 5 years old, helping them to learn their farm animals as they follow Luke on his adventure.

For more on LittleHouse go to

LITTLEHOUSELIVE.COM

Look Luke it's a Moo-cow

That's not a Moo-cow!
That's a Sheep

and it goes
"Bhaaaa"

Hey Luke that's a Moo-cow!

No that's a Donkey
and it goes "HeeHaw"

Look Luke! A Moo-cow!

That's not a Moo-cow!

That's a bunny
"Nuck Nuck Nuck"

Look at that big
Moo-cow!

Hey Luke it's a Moo-cow!

Awww, no it's
a barn cat.

"Meow"

Look at that crazy Moo-Cow

That's a Goat
and it goes "Bleat Bleat"

Luke, look at that Moo-cow

That's a Chicken.
It says,

"Cluck Cluck"

Look Luke
a Moo-cow!

A Moo-cow? NOOOO

That's a Dog!

"Woof"

Luke, over there a Moo-cow!

No thats a Rooster

It says
"Cocka-doodle-do"

Look Luke, finally a Moo-cow!!!

That's NOT a Moo-cow!!!
That's a Pig

it goes "Oink Oink"

Look Luke it's a
Moo, Moo Moo-cow!

That's **not** a Moo, Moo, Moo-cow

It's a
Cow!

"MOOOOOOOOO"

EXPECTING
Hot Tubbing Moms

Tips for Safe Relaxation

Pregnancy is a time filled with excitement, anticipation, and many questions. Expecting mothers often seek ways to relax and alleviate some of the discomforts that come with pregnancy. One common question is whether it's safe to use a hot tub during pregnancy. This article will explore the benefits, risks, and guidelines for using a hot tub while pregnant, ensuring you can make informed decisions for your health and your baby's.

BENEFITS OF HOT TUB USE DURING PREGNANCY

Relaxation and Stress Relief

Soaking in a hot tub can help reduce stress and promote relaxation. The warm water soothes tired muscles and can help alleviate the physical and mental stresses of pregnancy. The gentle, consistent heat can help your body unwind, making it easier to manage the various changes and challenges that come with carrying a baby.

Pain Relief

The buoyancy of the water helps reduce the pressure on joints and muscles, providing relief from common pregnancy aches, such as back pain and swollen feet. Pregnant women often experience discomfort due to the extra weight they carry, and the warm water can provide much-needed relief from this strain.

Improved Circulation

Immersing your body in warm water can improve blood flow and circulation. This enhanced circulation can help reduce swelling in your extremities and promote overall cardiovascular health, which is particularly beneficial during pregnancy when your body is working harder to support your growing baby.

Reduced Muscle Tension and Cramping

Pregnant women often experience muscle cramps and tension, especially in the legs. The heat and buoyancy of the water can help soothe and relax these muscles, reducing cramping and improving overall comfort.

Enhanced Mood and Mental Health

The calming effect of warm water can also have positive impacts on your mental health. Taking time to relax in a hot tub can help reduce anxiety and improve mood, contributing to overall mental well-being during pregnancy. The combination of physical relief and mental relaxation can make a significant difference in how you feel day-to-day.

Better Sleep

The relaxation achieved from a warm soak can promote better sleep, which is often elusive during pregnancy. Improved sleep quality can enhance overall health and well-being, making it easier to cope with the demands of pregnancy.

RISKS OF HOT TUB USE DURING PREGNANCY

Increased Body Temperature
One of the main concerns with hot tub use during pregnancy is the risk of hyperthermia (elevated body temperature). High temperatures can be harmful to the developing baby, particularly in the first trimester. Studies have shown that an increase in core body temperature above 101°F (38.3°C) can increase the risk of neural tube defects and other developmental issues.

Dehydration
Prolonged exposure to hot water can lead to dehydration, which is particularly concerning during pregnancy when your body requires more fluids to support your baby's development.

Blood Pressure Changes
The heat from a hot tub can cause your blood vessels to dilate, leading to a drop in blood pressure. This can result in dizziness or fainting, posing a risk to both you and your baby.

Guidelines for Safe Hot Tub Use During Pregnancy

Limit Time
Limit your time in the hot tub to 10-15 minutes to prevent your core body temperature from rising too high.

Monitor Temperature
Keep the hot tub temperature at or below 100°F (37.8°C). Some experts recommend keeping it even lower, around 98°F (36.7°C), to be extra cautious.

Avoid Early Pregnancy
Consider avoiding hot tub use during the first trimester when the risk of hyperthermia-related issues is highest.

Listen to Your Body
Pay attention to how you feel. If you start to feel overheated, dizzy, or uncomfortable, get out of the hot tub immediately.

Stay Hydrated
Drink plenty of water before, during, and after using the hot tub to stay hydrated.

Seek Medical Advice
Always consult your healthcare provider before using a hot tub during pregnancy. Your doctor can provide personalized advice based on your health and pregnancy.

Dearest Reader

It is with the utmost delight and gratitude that I extend my sincerest thanks for your time and attention spent perusing this most charming Hot Tub Lifestyle Guide. In an era where distractions abound and moments of tranquility are fleeting, your commitment to the pursuit of relaxation and well-being is both commendable and inspiring.

Throughout these pages, we have ventured together through the enchanting realms of hot tub bliss, uncovering secrets of mindfulness, discovering the pleasures of hydrotherapy, and indulging in the simple joys of a starry night soak. We have delved into the art of crafting the perfect hot tub cocktail, reveled in the laughter of a game night, and explored the benefits of yoga within the soothing embrace of warm waters.

As this guide draws to a close, it is my fervent wish that the knowledge and experiences shared herein have not only enlightened your mind but also enriched your heart. May you find countless opportunities to retreat into your personal oasis, where the bubbling waters whisper tales of serenity and the gentle steam carries away the cares of the day.

May your future soaks be filled with the blissful harmony of nature and luxury, and may each moment spent within the comforting depths of your hot tub bring you joy, peace, and renewal. Whether it is the soft glow of dawn, the golden hues of dusk, or the silvered canopy of night that accompanies your sojourns, may you always emerge refreshed and invigorated.

Thank you, dear reader, for embarking on this journey with me. It has been an honor to guide you through the myriad wonders of hot tub living. I bid you many happy soaks and tranquil moments, until we meet again in the pages of another tale.

Yours most sincerely,

Cindy Melbrod

CROSSWORD ANSWERS:

Across

2. JETS

3. ESCAPE

6. FAMILY

11. SWIMSUIT

12. MEDITATION

13. ZEN

14. AROMATHERAPY

15. WINE

17. HEAT

19. TRANQUIL

Down

1. TOWEL

2. JACUZZI

4. PARTY

5. LAUGHTER

7. MASSAGE

8. ROMANCE

9. STARGAZING

10. UNWIND

16. BUBBLES

18. BOUYANCY

WORD SEARCH ANSWERS

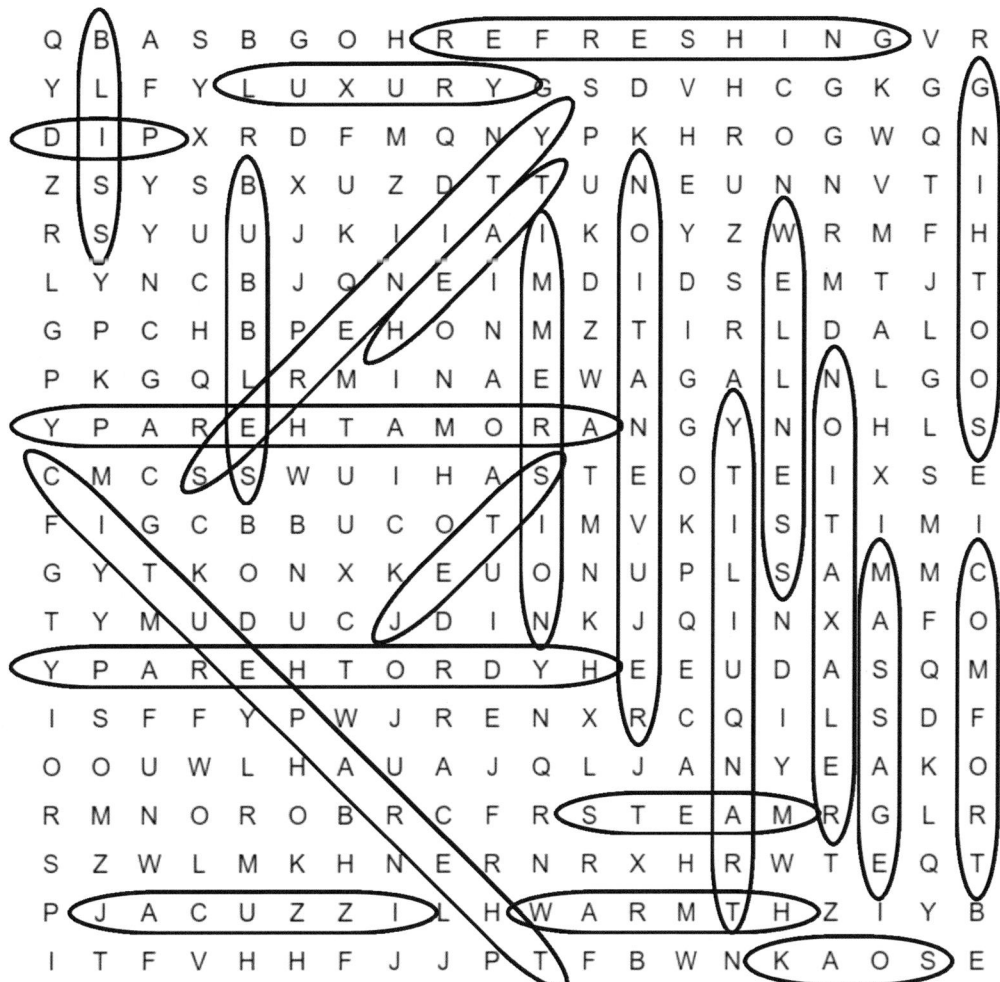

Acknowledgments

This book would not have come to life without the incredible support and encouragement of some truly special people. To my husband, whose steadfast belief in my vision has been invaluable. To my neighborhood friends, whose collective inspiration sparked many of the ideas and topics in this book. And to my industry friends and family, who stood by me with unwavering support throughout this journey.

Content Disclaimer

The photos included in this book are for illustrative purposes only and do not imply endorsement of any specific brands or products. This book does not provide detailed instructions for hot tub maintenance or care. For specific guidance on hot tub maintenance and care, please consult your hot tub manufacturer or a professional spa care provider.

Stay Connected

Thank you for exploring the hot tub lifestyle with me. For additional tips, inspiration, and resources, visit my website at www.cindymelbrod.com.

Liability Disclaimer

The content of this book is intended for informational and entertainment purposes only and should not be considered professional advice. The author and publisher assume no responsibility or liability for any injuries, damages, or losses incurred as a result of following the advice or information presented herein. Readers are encouraged to consult with healthcare professionals, legal advisors, or other relevant experts before engaging in any activities or making decisions based on the content of this book.

Stay Bubbly!

www.ingramcontent.com/pod-product-compliance
Lightning Source LLC
Chambersburg PA
CBRC091538260326
41914CB00022B/1649